Ultimate FACTIVITY Collection

LEGENDS OF CHIMA™

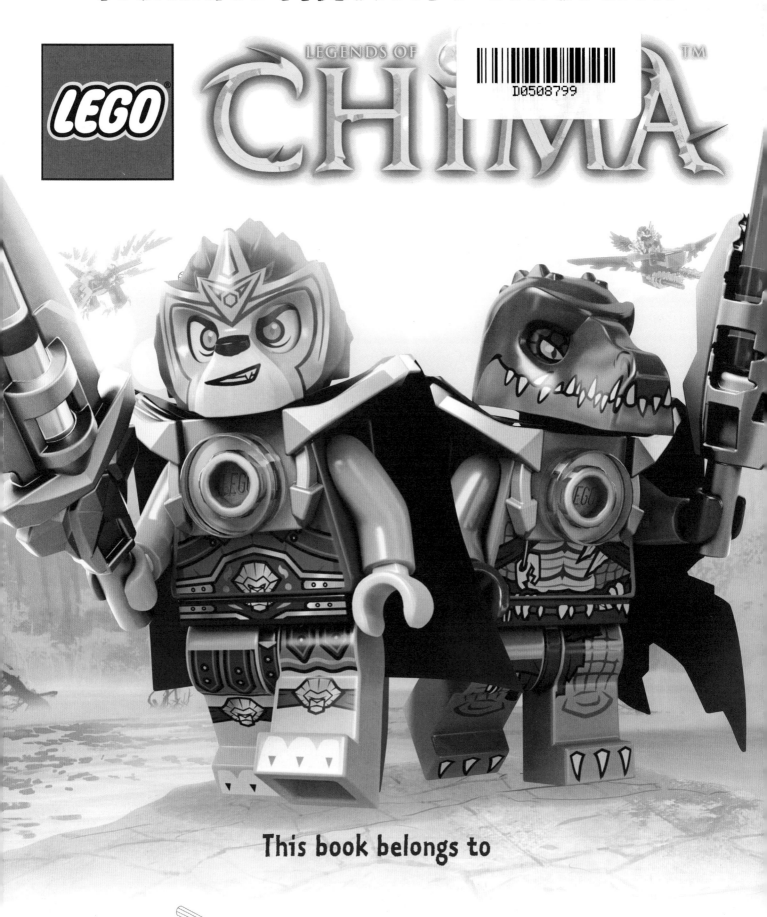

This book belongs to

_____

Welcome to Chima™

This beautiful kingdom is a natural paradise, but look a little closer and you will discover a few surprises. This is a mystical world where animals can walk and talk, just like humans! These amazing creatures strive for one thing: A magical power source called CHI.

Read the captions, then find the sticker that best fits the space.

Magical CHI

CHI looks a lot like water at first, but then it turns into blue glowing balls of light. CHI orbs give animals, and their weapons and vehicles, awesome power.

Cavora Falls

Mount Cavora is a beautiful floating mountain. It has a CHI-filled waterfall that flows into Chima™.

Power-up!

The animals plug CHI into special harnesses on their chests. The CHI boosts their natural animal abilities, and makes them faster and stronger.

Brave Lions

There are eight main tribes of animals in Chima. The Lion Tribe are the guardians of the CHI. They distribute CHI equally to each animal tribe.

Crafty Crocs

The Crocodiles are very greedy. They started a conflict among all the tribes when they demanded more CHI than everyone else.

Super vehicles

The animals drive special, super-fast vehicles called Speedorz™. Each Speedor has a wheel carved from TribeStone – a magical stone from Mount Cavora.

Courageous Eagles

The Eagle Tribe have joined forces with the Lions to protect the law. They also believe everyone should be given the same amount of CHI.

Naughty Wolves

The cunning Wolves think the Crocodiles have the right idea! They want to get their paws on as much CHI as they possibly can!

Fact Challenge

The Land of Chima

Go on a quest and explore Chima

Chima is a tropical paradise. The characterful homes of the animal tribes can be found deep within its beautiful jungles, grasslands, swamps and mountains. Today is CHI day, when all the animals gather at the golden Lion Temple.

The Quest

1. Grab a LEGO® minifigure, or something else to use as a counter, and place it at the start position.

2. Ask a friend to join you on your quest and decide who will go first.

3. Take turns to roll a die, then move the number of spaces that are shown on the die.

4. Be the first person to reach the Lion Temple for CHI day.

5. Watch out for hazards along the way!

Croc Swamp

The snapping gates on the Crocs' swamp hideout look like a ferocious, sharp-toothed croc jaw. They make it clear to visitors that only Crocs are welcome here.

24 A Raven sells you a rusty old Croc car. Hop in and whizz forward 2 spaces before it breaks down!

23

22 You find a secret stash of CHI orbs. Power up and move forward 5 spaces.

21

The Gorillas have formed a roadblock to protect a flower in the road. Miss a go while they save it.

Start

1

2

3 Two Crocs chase you out of Croc territory. Run forward 2 spaces, and make it snappy!

An eagle-eyed Eagle spots you from above and gives you directions. Move forward 2 spaces.

4

5

6

7

8

Ouch! You just slipped on a Gorilla's discarded banana skin. Go back 1 space.

Lion Temple

The Lions' gleaming temple is the pride of the tribe. Once a month, the Lions welcome other tribes here on CHI day, when they distribute CHI. However, if any tribes get too greedy, the lion-shaped gates will snap shut!

28

29

End

A Croc drops a weapon as he zooms past in his Claw Ripper. Grab it and go forward 2 spaces.

27

26

25

Is that a Predator Plant's vine wrapped around your leg? Get out of here! Go forward 2 spaces.

The Outlands

You won't find any of the tribes' homes here – but you will find flesh-eating Predator Plants! This dark, misty jungle zone is extremely dangerous.

18

19

17

20

A Rhino with poor eyesight accidentally rams into you and knocks you down. Move back 1 space.

16

Eagle Castle

The Eagles' quirky castle gives them a great vantage point over Chima. If any enemy tribes attack, they can launch an awesome aerial assault.

Worriz' Combat Lair

The Wolves like to roam around so their homes are mobile. Worriz' vicious vehicle is designed for combat on the move.

15

You trip over a Bear who is taking an afternoon nap. Jump forward 1 space.

14

You are held up when the Eagle King decides to tell you all about his philosophy on life. Miss a go.

13

The Wolves have picked up your scent. Go back 2 spaces and hide behind a tree.

9

10

11

12

The Power of CHI
Draw the CHI-up moment

CHI gives the animals a surge of power. It heightens their natural animal instincts and makes them faster and stronger. When the animals CHI-up, a large version of their inner warrior appears briefly behind them.

Plugging CHI
When animals plug CHI, the burst of power they feel lasts for a few hours. They are left feeling tired afterwards, so should only use it when absolutely necessary.

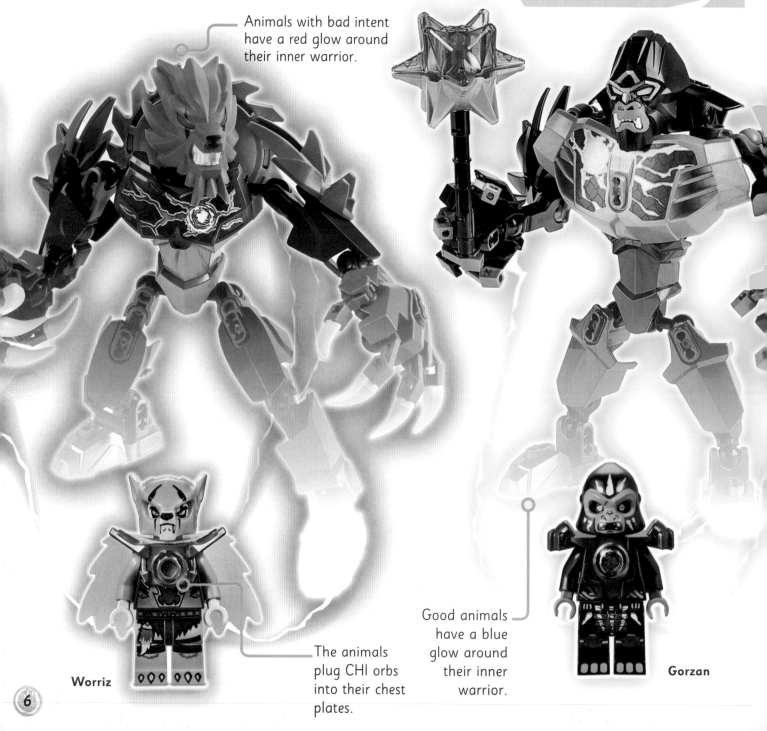

Animals with bad intent have a red glow around their inner warrior.

The animals plug CHI orbs into their chest plates.

Good animals have a blue glow around their inner warrior.

Worriz

Gorzan

Draw the inner warrior's **chest plate**.

What will the **shield** and **sword** look like?

Look at the other **inner warriors** for inspiration.

What colour will Laval's inner warrior glow?

Place a CHI orb sticker on Laval's chest and draw his inner warrior.

Laval

Guardians of CHI

Create a Lion Code scroll

Read about the Lion Code and fill in the blanks on the scroll. Next, decorate the scroll.

The Lions are the sacred guardians of CHI. They follow an important code to make sure there is a constant, balanced flow of CHI in Chima at all times. If this balance is upset, all kinds of natural disasters will strike.

CHI protectors

The Lions monitor the amount of CHI used by all the animal tribes. They have to make sure that there is never too much or too little CHI in the Sacred Pool of CHI. The Pool is located in the Lion Temple and is where CHI orbs are collected.

Lion Temple

Lion guards

CHI Day

At the monthly CHI Day, all the animals go to the Lion Kingdom where the Lions distribute the CHI equally to all tribes. Each tribe is given 50 CHI orbs — even enemy tribes! The Lions are bound by these rules and traditions. They follow the rules at all times.

King LaGravis

You could **decorate** the scroll with stickers or drawings of Lions, CHI or symbols.

The Lion Code

1 We, the Lions, must make sure that the Sacred Pool of CHI must never have too much or _____ _____ CHI.

2 We must always distribute the CHI _____ to all tribes.

3 Each tribe should be allocated _____ CHI orbs each month, even enemy tribes.

4 CHI should be given to the animal tribes in the Lion Kingdom on _____ _____ .

5 We must follow these rules at _____ _____ .

Find the **answers** on page 97.

Fact Challenge

Find the **sticker** of the **Lion's head seal** at the back of the book to seal the scroll.

Chima Conflict

Write in the speech bubbles

The tribes of Chima once lived in peace and harmony. Two of the animals, Lion Prince Laval and Crocodile Prince Cragger, were best friends – until the Crocodiles became greedy and wanted more CHI. Now, Chima is a battleground as the tribes fight for control of the CHI.

Decide what each character will say and write it in the blank speech bubbles.

You could write in **pencil** first and then use a **pen**.

Soon, all-out war breaks out between the two tribes!

Unleash the power of the CHI!

During the battle, Cragger's parents fall into the Gorge of Eternal Depth. Cragger must become king of the Crocodiles!

Cragger's evil sister, Crooler, convinces Cragger to attack the Lions so they can get more CHI.

Defeat the Lions and make our parents proud!

Chima soon becomes divided by tribes battling over CHI. Which side will win – good or bad?

More CHI for everyone! Hehehe!

The Grand Arena

Design a new racecourse

Speedor contests are held at the Grand Arena every month. Racers compete for the rare and extra-powerful Golden CHI orb. The Golden CHI is magical – it creates a new track and obstacle course for each contest!

Read about the Grand Arena obstacles. Next, add stickers to design your course. Then draw the track between the obstacles.

Whirling Vines

This gate has a vicious carnivorous plant over it that will snap up anything that gets too near!

Start

Find the Grand Arena **stickers** at the back of the book.

Croc Chomp

Racers need to drive quickly through this jaw-snapping gate, or the spiky teeth will come crashing down on them!

Ring of Fire

This obstacle challenges the competitors' agility. If they aren't careful they'll jump right into the flames!

How **long** is your **course** going to be?

Royal Roost

Crashing into this tower will cause its CHI to tumble onto the ground, where racers can grab it.

CHI Waterfall

Competitors need to aim at the swinging target if they want to win the CHI orb balancing above it.

Ice Tower

Knocking down this Ice Tower will reward a racer with a CHI orb to power up with!

Jungle Gates

Racers need to guide their Speedorz through the Jungle Gates as quickly as possible!

Where are your **obstacles** going to go?

Use a **pencil** to draw the **track** between the stickers.

Finish

13

The Legend Beasts
Complete the sticker jigsaw

The Legend Beasts are eight mysterious and mighty creatures who live in the Outlands. There is one for each of the original tribes, who for a long time didn't even believe that they were real. According to the stories, they have the power to save Chima if it comes under threat.

Read about some of the Legend Beasts, then use stickers to complete another Beast.

Lion Legend Beast

The Lion Beast is strong and brave, just like the Lion Tribe. It has a fear of water that Laval must help it overcome.

Eagle Legend Beast

Only two of the Legend Beasts can fly – the Eagle Beast and Raven Beast. The Eagle Beast is very intelligent and noble.

Crocodile Legend Beast

Cragger goes into battle riding the Crocodile Beast. Like the Crocodiles themselves, their Beast is very good at swimming.

Wolf Legend Beast

Worriz is the only Wolf who can understand the Wolf Beast's howl. For many years, the entire tribe has worshipped one of its teeth.

Into battle!

There is a **rider** sitting on the Legend Beast's **back**.

War cry

This Legend Beast may have a **fierce face**, but is actually a bit **groovy**...

Fact Challenge

Smashing power

The Legend Beast has a pair of **powerful fists**.

This Legend Beast is from the ✎ _____ Tribe.

It might look ferocious, but it is actually a bit ✎ _____.

It can smash things with its powerful ✎ _____.

Find the **answers** on page 97.

Chima Challenge

Test your knowledge on this section

Answer each question. If you need help, look back through the section.

Now you have finished the first section of the book, take the Chima Challenge to see if you are a true Chima expert!

 1. Find the sticker that best matches the description:

This grand building is where the animal tribes collect CHI each month.

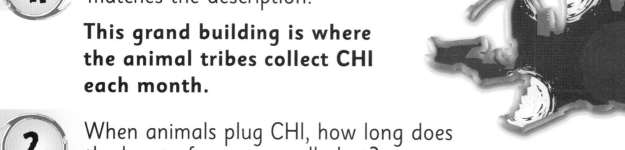

 2. When animals plug CHI, how long does the burst of power usually last?

five minutes ☐   **a few hours** ☐   **two weeks** ☐

 **3.** Cragger became king of the Crocodile Tribe because his parents disappeared into the Croc swamp.

True ☐   **False** ☐

 4. Name this Lion. ✏ _____

_____

 5. The winner of the Grand Arena race wins a

✏ _____ CHI orb.

Find the **answers** on page 97.

Now you have finished the Chima Challenge, reward yourself by filling this scene with stickers!

The Tribes of Chima

The animal tribes of Chima used to live in peace, but now battle rages across their magical land. The greedy Crocodiles are battling the Lions for control of the precious CHI. The Wolves, Eagles, Ravens and Gorillas have all taken sides. Who will triumph?

Read the captions, then find the sticker that best fits the space.

Fighting together
The valiant Lions fight side by side with the Eagles. They battle against the crafty Crocs and their allies.

The bad guys
The Crocodiles lead their allies – the Wolves and Ravens. What started as a feud between the Lions and Crocs has become a far greater conflict.

The Raven Tribe
The Ravens just can't resist the urge to steal things, whether they are valuable or not. Ravens are smooth talkers, but can also be vicious fighters.

Animal kings

Some – but not all – of the tribes in Chima are ruled by kings. King LaGravis rules the Lions, while King Crominus leads the Crocs.

Croc twins

Prince Cragger rules the Crocs after his father disappears. He is often tricked and controlled by his evil twin sister, Crooler.

The Rhino Tribe

The Rhinos are among the strongest creatures in all of Chima. They are not very bright and are easily controlled by the Crocs.

The Gorilla Tribe

The Gorillas are the Lions' most powerful allies, but their laid-back attitude makes it hard to get them involved!

Friendly animals

Not all of the animals in Chima belong to the main tribes. There are also Skunks, Foxes, Beavers and many others. They usually avoid taking sides.

Fact Challenge

The Lion Tribe

Spot the tribe members

The noble Lions are the sworn guardians of the CHI. All Lions are fair and like to follow rules, which they take *very* seriously. But no Lion is the same as another — there are many differences!

Read about the tribe members. Then use the clues to identify each Lion.

Lennox

Young Lennox is a fearless foot soldier. He loves speeding around Chima in his "Lion Attack" vehicle.

Laval

Prince Laval is brave but headstrong. One day he will be king of the Lion Tribe.

Longtooth

This old Lion soldier looks like he has been in many battles. He enjoys telling long stories about all the action.

Leonidas

Orange-haired Leonidas is a foot soldier and guard. Be careful what you ask him to do — he is easily confused!

I wear a plain blue head decoration.

I am often described as dopey.

I have a toothy smile.

Find our **stickers** at the back of the book.

1 My name is:

_____

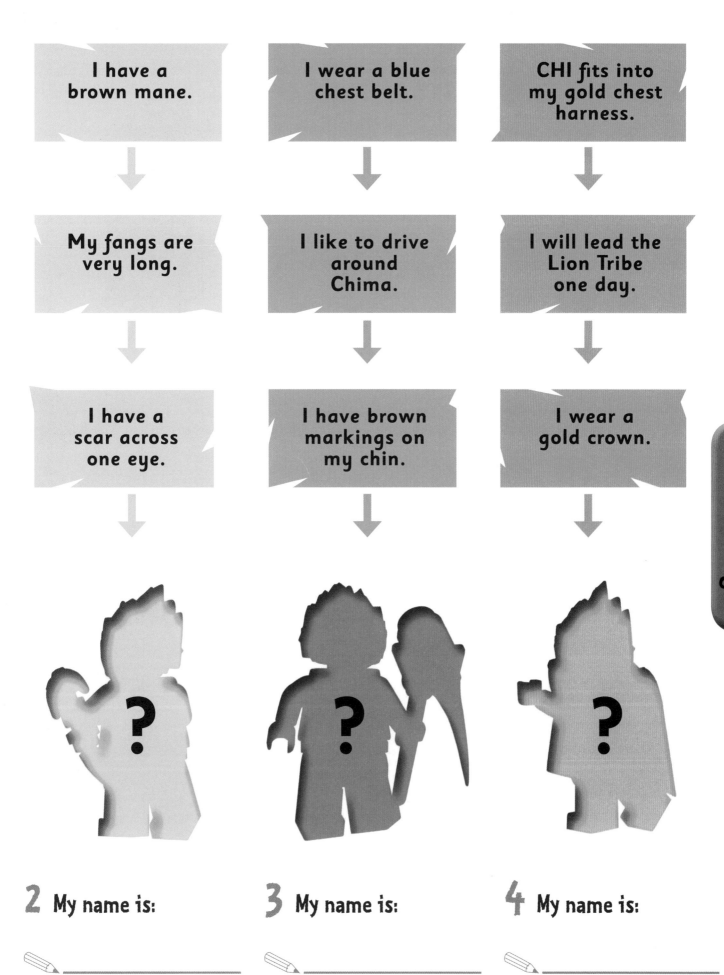

I have a
brown mane.

↓

My fangs are
very long.

↓

I have a
scar across
one eye.

↓

2 My name is:
✎ _____

I wear a blue
chest belt.

↓

I like to drive
around
Chima.

↓

I have brown
markings on
my chin.

↓

3 My name is:
✎ _____

CHI fits into
my gold chest
harness.

↓

I will lead the
Lion Tribe
one day.

↓

I wear a
gold crown.

↓

4 My name is:
✎ _____

Fact Challenge

Find the **answers** on page 97.

The Crocodile Tribe

Write a short story about Leonidas escaping the Crocs

The Crocs are a tough gang of sly and slippery villains. They live deep in the heart of the swamp. It is a menacing place, which is perfect for the sneaky Crocs! Their hideout has a hanging cell where they hold their enemies.

Read about the Crocs, who take it in turns to guard Leonidas in their cell. Then decide which guard Leonidas can escape from.

There is no right or wrong answer!

Leonidas in the hanging cell

Find the **sticker** at the back of the book.

Leonidas escapes the cell

The Croc guard that Leonidas escapes from is:

_____

How Leonidas escapes:

_____

_____

_____

_____

_____

Crominus

King Crominus is the tough leader of the Crocs. He is **sensible**. Although he does not like the Lions, he **respects** them.

Crawley

Crawley is one of Cragger's henchmen. He uses his tail as a whip-like weapon to trap victims. He can be **jumpy** and **nervous**.

Crooler

Cragger's twin sister is sly and cunning. She secretly tricks Cragger into doing what she wants. She is always **very busy** making naughty plans.

Cragger

Prince Cragger is the son of Crominus. He is always **greedy** for CHI. Cragger was once **friends** with the Lions, but they are now his enemies.

Crug

Crug the thug is a loyal foot soldier of the tribe, but he is **not the cleverest** Croc! He follows Cragger's orders without question.

The Eagle Tribe
Design a new Eagle vehicle

The Eagles have a reputation for having their heads in the clouds, but they are actually great thinkers and inventors. Their technology and vehicles are the most advanced in all of Chima.

Read about the Eagles and their vehicles, then design a new vehicle for Ewar or Ewald.

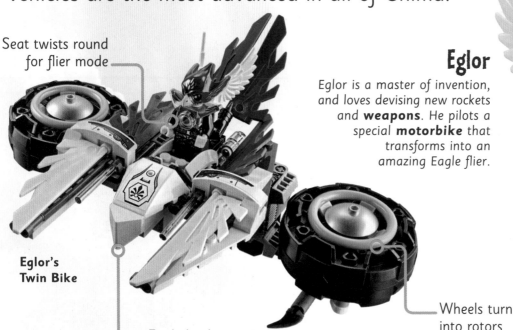

Seat twists round for flier mode

Eglor's Twin Bike

Eagle beak decoration

Wheels turn into rotors

Eglor

Eglor is a master of invention, and loves devising new rockets and **weapons**. He pilots a special **motorbike** that transforms into an amazing Eagle flier.

Eglor

Eris

Eris

Eris is very intelligent and quick-witted. She loves **adventure** and **puzzles**, and she has a **lightning-fast** vehicle to suit her fearless personality.

Feathers help with agility

Detachable cockpit

Eris's Eagle Interceptor

Ewar

Ewar is a brave warrior. He likes to fly **small**, **speedy** vehicles to stop other tribes from stealing the Eagles' CHI.

Ewald

Ewald is the king of the Eagle Tribe, and also Eris's father. As king, his vehicles would be **big** and **grand**, and possibly **chauffeur**-driven.

The new Eagle vehicle is called:

_____

Most Eagle vehicles have **feathers**, **wings** or a **beak**.

Eagle vehicles are usually coloured **blue** and **gold**.

Does your vehicle **fly** or **drive** fast along the ground?

Has your vehicle got any **weapons** or other **gadgets**?

The Wolf Tribe

Find the Wolves and their home

The Wolves love to battle, and are fearsome fighters. They prefer to move in packs, and don't like it when the tribe is split up. They live together in a mobile Combat Lair.

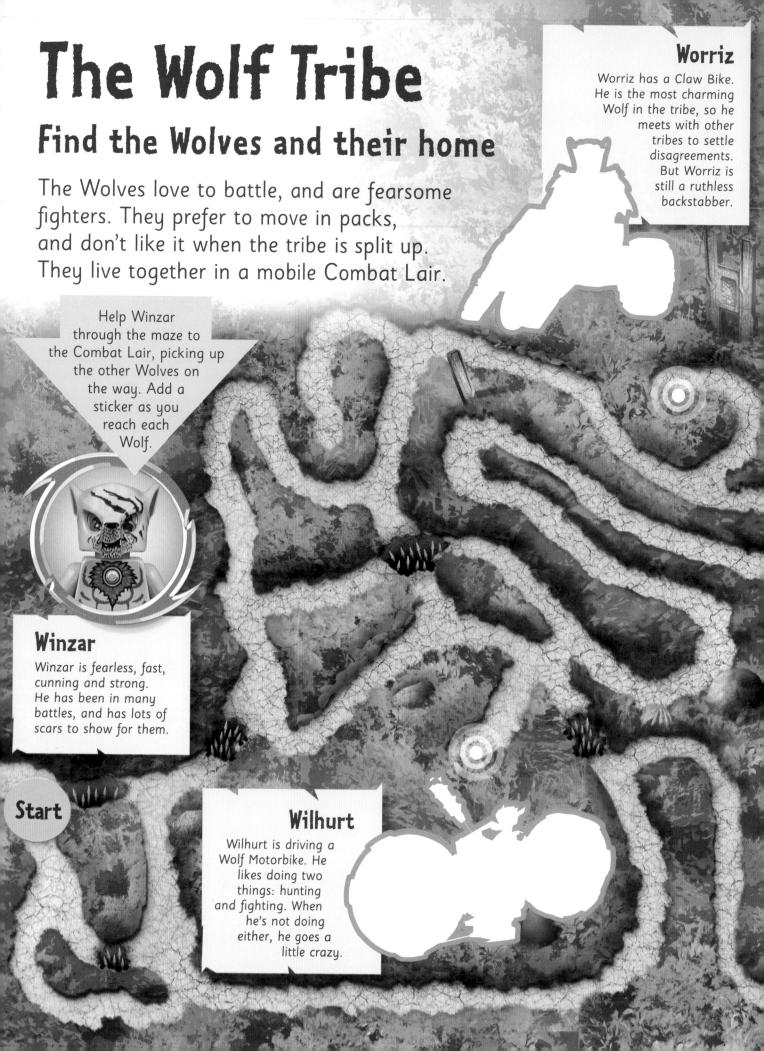

Worriz

Worriz has a Claw Bike. He is the most charming Wolf in the tribe, so he meets with other tribes to settle disagreements. But Worriz is still a ruthless backstabber.

Help Winzar through the maze to the Combat Lair, picking up the other Wolves on the way. Add a sticker as you reach each Wolf.

Winzar

Winzar is fearless, fast, cunning and strong. He has been in many battles, and has lots of scars to show for them.

Start

Wilhurt

Wilhurt is driving a Wolf Motorbike. He likes doing two things: hunting and fighting. When he's not doing either, he goes a little crazy.

End

Combat Lair

The Combat Lair is the Wolves' home. It has six huge wheels to carry it over rough terrain. It can break up into five smaller vehicles to fight off attacks, and it has a prison to hold captured enemies.

Windra

Windra pilots a Wolf Helicopter. She looks soft and cuddly, but underneath her fluffy exterior lurks a cruel heart and a vicious fighter.

Wakz

Wakz is also riding a Claw Bike. He is one of the oldest Wolves, and is cunning and ferocious. Wakz is not afraid of using overwhelming force against his enemies.

The Gorilla Tribe

Draw a new Gorilla

The Gorillas are the allies of the Lions and Eagles. They are the strongest warriors in Chima, but they would much rather relax than fight. It takes Gorillas a while to get involved in combat, but when they do, watch out!

Read about the Gorillas. Then design a new member of their Tribe.

Gordo
Gordo is a thoughtful leader. He has a sun pattern on his forehead and he wears impressive chest and shoulder armour plates.

Gorzan
Gorzan is kind and caring, and loves nature. He wears a belt of twisted vines and he has stripey green markings on his fur.

G'Loona
Gorzan's sister decorates her fur with pretty flowers and leaves. Like her brother, she wears a CHI pendant around her neck.

Grizzam
Striking white Grizzam is friends with Gorzan and G'Loona. He wears knee pads to protect him when swinging from tree to tree.

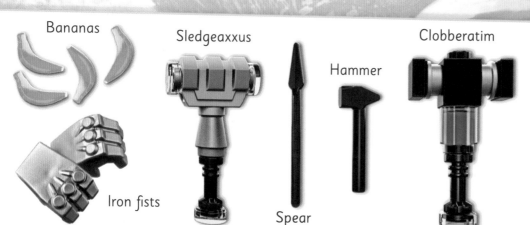

Bananas

Sledgeaxxus

Hammer

Clobberatim

Iron fists

Spear

Gorillas' weapons
The Gorillas prefer peace to war, but in combat they shoot bananas at their enemies. When more powerful weapons are needed, they use different types of hammers. They also have iron fists for frightening foes.

You could add a **pattern**, such as **stripes**.

What **colour** will your Gorilla be?

Draw a **weapon** in your Gorilla's hand, too!

How about adding a **plant** or **flower** decoration?

This Gorilla is called:  _____

The Raven Tribe

Find the Ravens and their hidden loot

Watch out for the Ravens! These sneaky animals love stealing from the other tribes. They will do anything and everything to get their greedy hands on some precious "treasure".

Read the captions about the Ravens and find the sticker that best fits the space.

Rawzom

The Grand Thief Master of the Raven Tribe wears a gold crown. He is a very skilled tracker and finds all kinds of treasure, including precious CHI.

?

Find the **stickers** at the back of the book.

Lions' CHI

How many stolen objects can you find in the forest? Write the numbers in the boxes.

Razar

The prince of the tribe has a hook hand, which is great for swiping small treasures like tasty bananas. Naughty Razar then sells them back to the Gorillas, of course!

?

Gorillas' banana

Razcal

Gold-beaked Razcal is the Raven Tribe's accountant. He keeps track of everything the Ravens steal, including other tribes' weapons.

?

Eagles' axe

Rizzo

Rizzo has a metal peg-leg and a matching eye patch. He will steal from anyone – even his so-called friends, the Wolves.

?

Wolves' Slizar

Find the **answers** on page 97.

Find the **answers** on page 97.

Fact Challenge

31

Chima Challenge

Test your knowledge on this section

Answer each question. If you need help, look back through the section.

Now you have finished the second section of the book, take the Chima Challenge to prove your Chima knowledge!

1. Find the sticker that best matches the description:

This menacing six-wheeled vehicle is also a home for one of the tribes.

2. Crawley is...

King of the Crocs   **Cragger's brother**   **Cragger's henchman**

3. The Eagles fight against the Gorillas.

True ☐   **False** ☐

4. Name this Raven. ✏ _____

5. Eglor rides a special ✏ _____ that can be transformed into an Eagle flier.

Find the **answers** on page 97.

Now you have finished the Chima Challenge, reward yourself by filling this scene with stickers!

Test your Knowledge

A New Threat

Dark and dangerous times have fallen on Chima!
The sacred waters from Mount Cavora have dried up,
and the animals can no longer collect CHI. With no
source of energy, the tribes will have to learn how
to work together if they want to save their home.

Read the captions, then find the sticker that best fits the space.

Find the **stickers** at the back of the book.

Dark days

Mount Cavora's beautiful CHI-filled waterfall has stopped flowing. A mysterious black cloud hovers ominously in the skies above.

Stolen CHI

Everybody wants to get their claws on the CHI now that it is so hard to find! The new bad guys are trying to steal all the orbs for themselves.

Outlands villains

Strange new faces are being spotted in Chima. The wicked Spider, Scorpion and Bat Tribes come from the hazardous Outlands in search of CHI.

Friend or foe?

Laval and Cragger must put their old arguments aside and join forces to rescue Chima before it's too late. Will they become true friends again?

Firm friends

Eris and Rogon become allies, despite the fact she is incredibly smart and he is very dumb. Rogon is actually in love with Eris!

Legend Beasts

The tribes of Chima are desperate to find the Legend Beasts. Only they have the power to make the Cavora Falls flow again.

Lavertus

Lavertus is a mysterious exile, who has lived alone in the Outlands for many years. The Chima Tribes are not sure if he's good or bad.

Spider Speedor

The Outlands Tribes all drive upgraded Speedorz. Each tribe creates their own menacing design.

A Team of Heroes

Design a shield for the new team

The battling tribes have put aside their differences to save their beautiful land. One brave member of each tribe has been selected to go into the scary Outlands. The mismatched band of animals need to come together. A new team shield will unite them!

Design a shield for the team. Try to represent the six team members in your design.

Razar the Raven

Sly Razar has a hook hand, sharp beak and sneaky-looking eyes. He has striking black wings and purple and black feathers.

Gorzan the Gorilla

Gorzan may not look like it, but he is a sensitive soul! He loves flowers and has a belt of twisted vines.

Eris the Eagle

Eris has majestic white wings. She wears a gold tiara and harness and gold feather-style armour.

Laval the Lion

Adventurous Prince Laval wears blue and gold royal armour with Lion head logos.

Worriz the Wolf

Worriz has been in many fights. He has lots of scratches, tattered grey clothes and very sharp fangs.

Cragger the Crocodile

Cragger has scales, lots of teeth and he wears a red robe. He has decorated his armour with teeth and bones.

Into the Outlands

The team must head into the Outlands, where they will face flesh-eating plants and dangerous animal tribes. They will need new shields to protect themselves!

Draw a **blue CHI orb** in the centre.

How about adding Eagle **wings** or Crocodile **teeth** to your design?

Look at the animals' **colours**, **armour** and **weapons** for inspiration.

The Outlands

Design an Outlands warning poster

The Outlands is a dark, treacherous jungle growing on poisonous soil. The plants and animals that live in the Outlands have become twisted and savage. Those who are foolish enough to enter this sinister realm rarely return...

Read about the Outlands, then add stickers to the poster and fill in the blanks.

The Outlands tribes

The evil tribes of the Outlands have joined together to form a great army. Led by the scary Scorpions, the clever Spiders and tough Bats fight to control Chima.

Predator plants

One of the greatest dangers in the Outlands is the carnivorous plant life. One false move is all it takes to get snapped up and eaten!

Terrible traps

The Spider Tribe have filled the Outlands with poisonous traps and webs. These will catch anyone who trespasses into their creepy cavern.

Vicious vehicles

The Outlands tribes have designed their vehicles to be terrifying, poisonous and almost impossible to escape from – just like the land where they live.

Add **stickers** of dangerous plants, animals, traps and vehicles.

You could add the words **"Danger!"** or **"Warning!"** at the top.

Find the **stickers** at the back of the book.

Enter the Outlands at your own risk! There are deadly

✎_____ plants and dangerous Bats,

Spiders and ✎_____tribes. Trespassers

will be caught in ✎_____ and chased away

by vicious ✎_____. Beware!

Find the **answers** on page 97.

The Scorpion Tribe
Draw the weapons on the vehicle

The Scorpions are the most powerful and aggressive of the Outlands tribes. They are leading the other tribes in their attack on Chima. Scorpions use their powerful tails to club and sting their opponents, and their vehicles carry terrifying poisonous weapons.

Draw the scary claws and stinger to go on King Scorm's Stinger vehicle.

King Scorm

King Scorm is very evil and very impatient. He wants to conquer all of Chima as fast as possible. He uses his tail to strike his henchmen if they displease him.

Scutter

Scutter has six legs and is incredibly strong and powerful. He carries a massive Sting Hammer, and his tail can shoot toxic blasts.

Scolder

Scolder is one of King Scorm's countless Scorpion foot soldiers. He is a tireless and obedient warrior.

Scorpion Stinger

Scorm's Scorpion Stinger is one of
the most powerful vehicles ever built
in Chima. It can attack using its
enormous claws and pincers, or use
its giant stinger and poison balls
to totally destroy its targets.

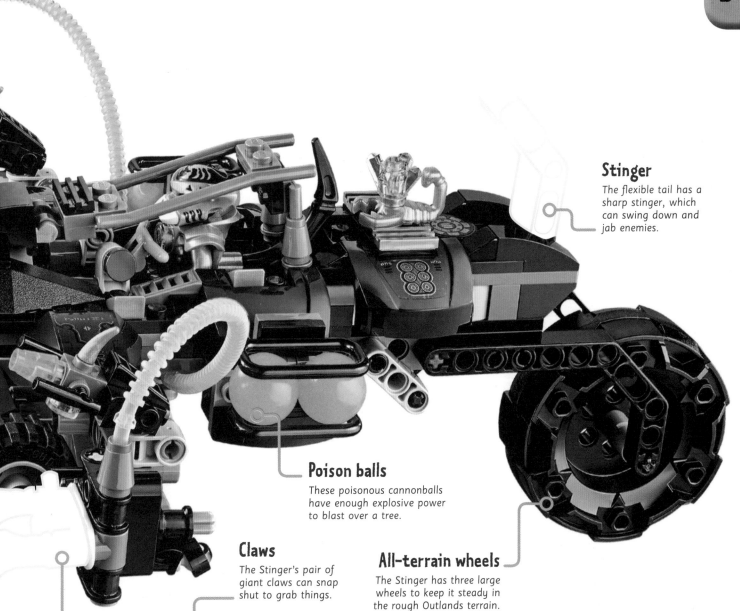

Stinger
The flexible tail has a
sharp stinger, which
can swing down and
jab enemies.

Poison balls
These poisonous cannonballs
have enough explosive power
to blast over a tree.

Claws
The Stinger's pair of
giant claws can snap
shut to grab things.

All-terrain wheels
The Stinger has three large
wheels to keep it steady in
the rough Outlands terrain.

The Spider Tribe
Complete Laval's Spider spy notes

The Spiders are the smartest of the Outlands tribes. As well as being loyal servants to their "beautiful" queen, Spiders are master engineers and builders. Their webs are as strong as steel. They use them to craft creepy structures and to tangle up their enemies.

Read about the Spiders. Then, finish Laval's notes and draw a picture of Queen Spinlyn.

Laval's mission

Laval has crept into Spider Canyon on a secret mission to find out more about this mysterious new foe.

Spinlyn's Cavern

Deep in Spider Canyon lies Queen Spinlyn's Cavern. It is a dark, dangerous place, full of icky webs and poisonous fangs. Be careful not to get caught!

Sparacon

Sparacon is the strongest Spider soldier. He is a cold, emotionless fighter. Like other Spider soldiers, he has four legs on his back.

Sparratus

Sparratus is a tough drone. He doesn't have any extra legs on his back, so he is very jealous of the Spider soldiers.

Spinlyn

Queen Spinlyn thinks she is irresistible, and the other Spiders all agree. She spends most of her time staring at her own hideous reflection.

Fill in the **blanks** to show what Laval has discovered about the Spiders.

Laval's Spider Notes

I have been watching the Spiders from my hiding place for quite a while now. They are a very odd tribe!

1 The Spiders are ruled by ✎_____ who thinks she is beautiful, but actually she is ✎_____ She lives in a dark ✎_____ in Spider Canyon.

2 The Spiders are very good at building things. They use their ✎_____ to make traps, cages and structures.

3 The other two types of Spider are Spider ✎_____ who have legs on their backs, and Spider ✎_____ who don't have legs on their backs.

I have drawn a little sketch of the Spider Queen:

Find the **answers** on page 97.

Fact Challenge

The Bat Tribe

Complete the Bat pictures

The Bats are not as strong as the Scorpions and Spiders, but they make up for it with sheer numbers. They attack as an overwhelming mass, hidden in a dense black cloud. Their greatest weakness is their lack of intelligence...

Read about the Bats, then draw and colour in the parts hidden by the cloud.

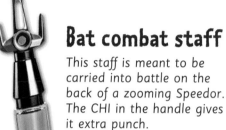

Bat combat staff

This staff is meant to be carried into battle on the back of a zooming Speedor. The CHI in the handle gives it extra punch.

Braptor

Braptor is mean and tough. Although he can't see very well, he has fantastic hearing, and can listen in on distant conversations.

Blista

Blista is strong, but prefers to use his lightning speed in battle. He claims that he always has his best ideas when he's hanging upside down.

Blista's Spikorr

Blista's personal weapon is called the Spikorr. It is decorated with fearsome green spikes.

Blista's Speedor

The Bats' Speedorz are sleek and fast, built to charge in and steal CHI before anyone is able to react. They have Bat-like wings to give them a scarier appearance.

Wing Striker cannons

What deals more damage than one cannon? Two cannons stuck together! These weapons are usually found on the side of a Wing Striker vehicle.

The Bats travel together as a massive **dark cloud**.

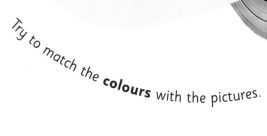

Try to match the **colours** with the pictures.

Battle for CHI

Finish the comic strip

The scary Outlands tribes are always on the look-out for more CHI to steal. It's a good thing the brave Lions are around to stop them in their creepy tracks!

Draw lightly with a **pencil** before you use **coloured pens** or pencils.

Read the story and then write and draw the ending.

Use these images to help you.

G'Loona the Gorilla

Happy, nature-loving G'Loona decorates her **brown** fur with **plants**.

Sparratus the Spider

Sparratus is very **scary**. He has huge **fangs** and mean eyes.

G'Loona the Gorilla is happily tending the plants in her garden when Sparratus the Spider races through in his vehicle, squashing everything!

Sparratus has stolen the Lions' CHI!

But Lennox is not far behind on his Speedor.

Sparratus turns and drives straight at Lennox.

But Lennox has an unlikely secret weapon — one of G'Loona's bananas!

He throws the slippery banana under Sparratus's wheels...

Spider Vehicle

This vehicle has nasty brown **Spider's legs** on the sides and **green** fangs on the front.

Orb of CHI

Orbs of CHI glow **blue**.

Lennox the Lion

Lennox is brave and very **strong**. He has a **brown mane** and wears **blue armour**.

Lennox's Speedor

This Speedor is **yellow** with **spiky weapons** attached to the back.

THE END!

How will the story **end**? You **decide**!

Chima Challenge

Test your knowledge on this section

Answer each question. If you need help, look back through the section.

Now you have finished the third section of the book, take the Chima Challenge to find out if you are a master of CHI!

1. Find the sticker that best matches the description:

This giant vehicle is driven by the Scorpion king.

2. Which of these are found in the Outlands?

Evil tribes ☐　**Giant rats** ☐　**Predator plants** ☐

3. The Spider Tribe is ruled by a king.

True ☐　　**False** ☐

4. Name this Bat. ✎ _____

5. Sparacon has four ✎ _____ on his back.

Now you have finished the Chima Challenge, reward yourself by filling this scene with stickers!

Test your Knowledge

Vehicles and Weapons

The tribes of Chima use CHI to power their awesome technology. Each tribe designs its own amazing vehicles and weapons – the Lions' vehicles feature Lions' faces, while the Rhinos' vehicles have horns. Across Chima, warriors carry mighty CHI-powered weapons into battle.

Read the captions, then find the sticker that best fits the space.

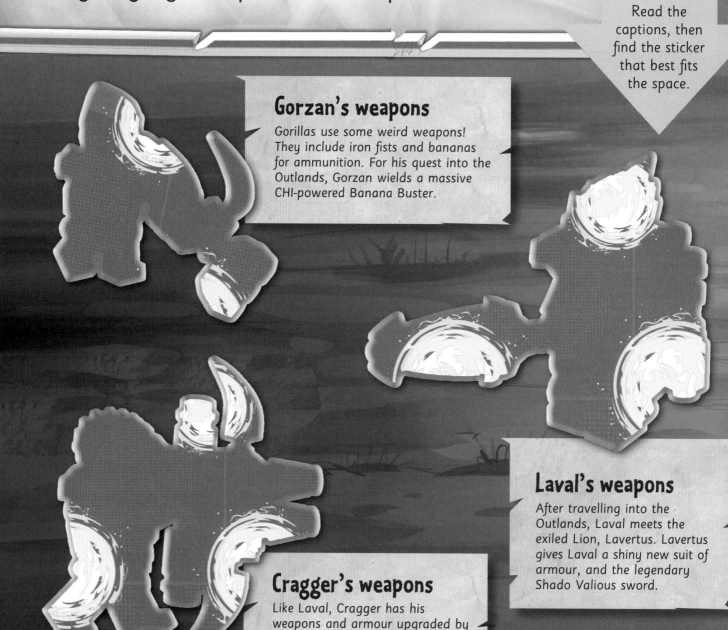

Gorzan's weapons

Gorillas use some weird weapons! They include iron fists and bananas for ammunition. For his quest into the Outlands, Gorzan wields a massive CHI-powered Banana Buster.

Laval's weapons

After travelling into the Outlands, Laval meets the exiled Lion, Lavertus. Lavertus gives Laval a shiny new suit of armour, and the legendary Shado Valious sword.

Cragger's weapons

Like Laval, Cragger has his weapons and armour upgraded by Lavertus. His new weapon is called Scale Ripper. It has huge fangs on either end, and blasts out CHI.

Sparratus's Spider Stalker

This menacing Spider vehicle shoots nasty webs to trap its targets. The front is built to look like a Spider's mouth, with vicious poisonous fangs.

Lennox's Lion Attack

Lennox's Lion Attack is built to charge right into battle. Like other Lion vehicles, its weapons and armour all face forward, as no Lion would ever run away from an enemy.

Speedorz

The tribes of Chima use their Speedor vehicles to compete in lightning-fast races and perilous jousting competitions.

Eris's weapons

Eris uses Eagle weapons that are graceful as well as effective. Her hammer has a sharp golden beak and white wing decoration.

Rogon's Rock Flinger

Rhino vehicles are bulky and tough, just like their drivers. They aren't very sophisticated, but make up for it with their brute strength and power.

Fact Challenge

51

Super Speedorz™
Design new Speedorz

Speedorz are used for travelling around Chima and for racing. The animals design and make their own unique Speedorz.

Look at these Speedorz to get ideas for designing your own.

Every Speedor is **decorated** to look like its **owner**.

Eagle Speedor

Equila's Speedor is called a **Skreekor 360**. The front is shaped like an Eagle's head, so it cuts through the air, just like an Eagle does.

All Speedorz have **one large wheel**.

This Speedor is called a

_____

What sort of **animals** are going to **drive** your Speedorz?

Wolf Speedor

Worriz has attached turbo jets to the back of his Speedor to make it zoom extra fast! His Speedor is called a **Frontor**.

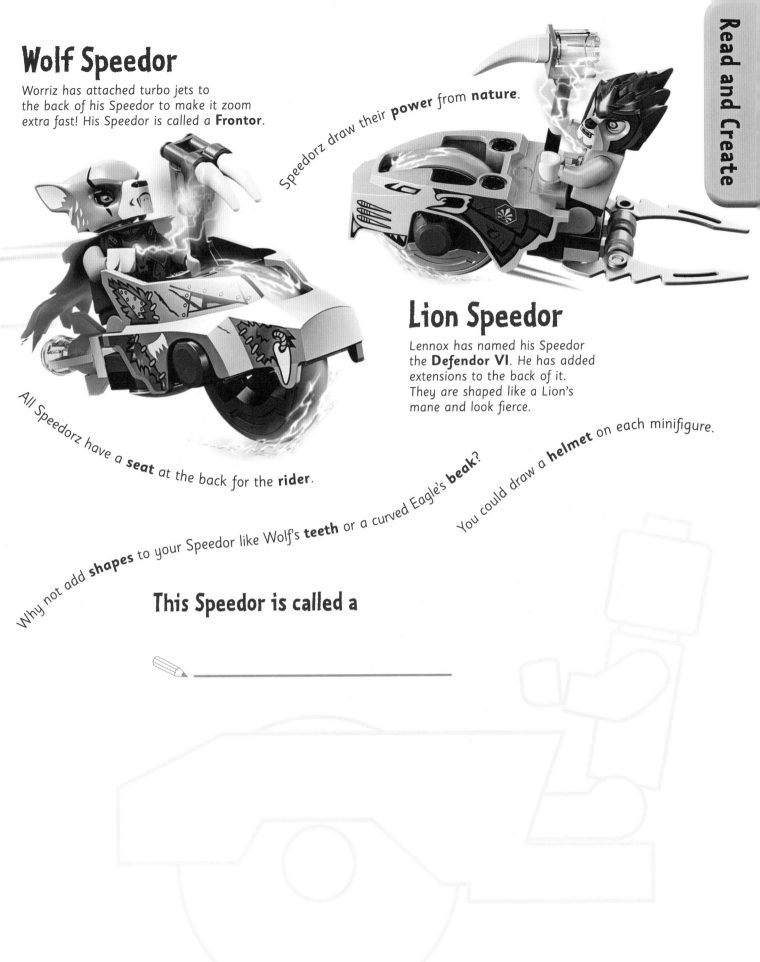

Speedorz draw their **power** from **nature**.

Lion Speedor

Lennox has named his Speedor the **Defendor VI**. He has added extensions to the back of it. They are shaped like a Lion's mane and look fierce.

All Speedorz have a **seat** at the back for the **rider**.

Why not add **shapes** to your Speedor like Wolf's **teeth** or a curved Eagle's **beak**?

You could draw a **helmet** on each minifigure.

This Speedor is called a

_____

Weapons Master
Match the weapon to its owner

An animal's choice of weapon is an expression of their personality and fighting style, as well as showing which tribe they belong to.

Work out which weapon belongs to each animal. Next, draw the weapon in the animal's hand.

Worriz

Worriz handles deals for the Wolf Tribe. His **sharp-fanged staff** signals to other tribes that he is a tough talker.

Razar

This greedy Raven **steals** weapons, but his favourite one is homemade. The **winged weapon** looks like its owner a little!

Maulus

The two white **fangs** on this fierce weapon look just like its owner's teeth. They are a symbol of the **pack** it was made by.

Swampvinus

The **snapping vine** on this staff is as fast and as powerful as a thrashing tail! Its red CHI crystal is fit for a **king**.

Eglaxxor

This **very old** CHI-powered **axe** can **fly through the air** at great speed, just like its owner.

Equila

Flying ace Equila dive bombs his enemies with his **double-bladed axe**! He is the guardian of his ancient weapon.

Crominus

The logical king of the Croc Tribe doesn't believe in fighting, but his **whipping weapon** shows he's no pushover, either.

LaGravis

The **noble king** of the Lion Tribe carries a **sword**. It has been passed down through the Lion heirs.

Find the **answers** on page 97.

Royal Valious

Only **great leaders** can use this weapon. It is made from an indestructible metal called Leochium. Its **royal** CHI crystal makes it extremely powerful.

Thundax

Cover your ears! The Thundax fires out a deafening shriek. This staff is built entirely from **stolen metal**. Its hand-painted blades look like **wings**.

Lavertus's Lair

Design a new base defence system

Lavertus was exiled from the Lion Tribe when Laval was very young. He now lives in a secret base deep in the dangerous Outlands, which he calls "The Lair". He has survived by inventing incredible new vehicles and weapons in his workshop. Lavertus is one talented Lion!

Read about Lavertus's inventions, then design something to help him defend his base.

Bat attack!

Blista the Bat is trying to get inside the base. How will Lavertus stop him?

Periscope

Lavertus invented this periscope to watch the Outlands from the safety of his Lair. He can see enemies coming from far away.

Gatling gun

Lavertus's massive gatling gun unleashes rapid-fire bursts of CHI. It's perfect against fast-moving targets.

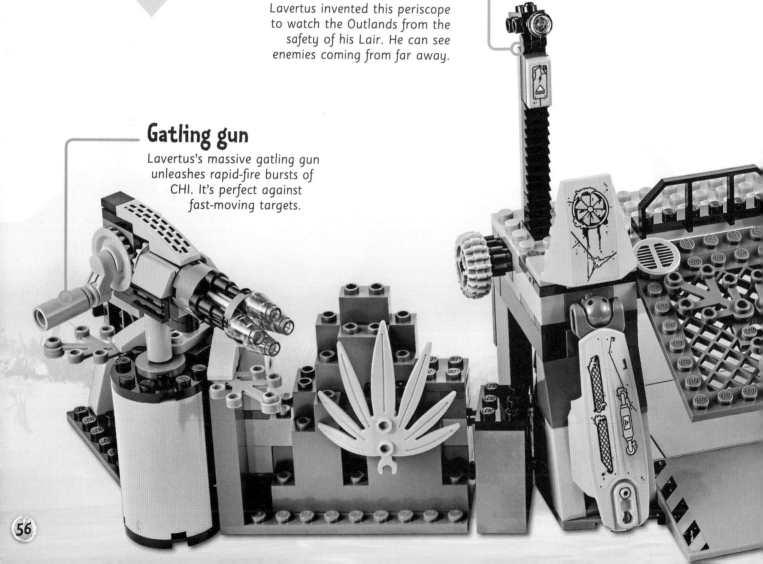

Is your invention a type of **weapon**, **spy system** or **trap**?

The new defence system is: ✎ _____

Does your invention *fire* CHI?

Scanner

This scanner can track any movement outside the base.

Is it on **top** of the wall, or **in front**?

Sentry gun

Lavertus designed the sentry gun to automatically fire at enemies who get too close to his front gate.

Workshop tools

Lavertus has lots of tools in his workshop. These help him to design and build his inventions.

Lavertus

The Outlands are a harsh place. Lavertus uses his inventions to keep himself safe. He carries a MaCHIgun when he goes outside the gate.

Front gate

This sturdy gate is camouflaged with plants to keep it hidden.

Ultra Striker

Complete the sticker jigsaw

The Eagles' awesome battle machine rolls along on huge tracks and is fitted with terrifying rocket shooters. The clever Eagles have even built in a detachable shuttle, so they can soar away from danger.

Tail fin
This tail fin looks like a bird's tail. It helps the Striker to travel very fast – like a soaring Eagle.

Use the stickers of the Striker parts to put together the vehicle.

CHI power cable
The cables link the CHI crystals to the rocket shooters to power them.

Shuttle
The Striker has an ejection system to launch the small shuttle from the rest of the Striker. Equila uses the shuttle to dive-bomb his enemies or to flee trouble.

Rocket shooter
When Equila is in combat, he fires rockets at his enemies from each side of the Striker.

Find the **stickers** at the back of the book.

The Striker was invented by Eglor, the Eagle genius.

Cockpit
Equila controls the Striker from the cockpit. He is the Eagles' flying ace, so likes it best when he launches the flying shuttle.

Folded wings
The blue wings look like an Eagle's. Two of the wings open out to fly the shuttle.

Rubber tracks
The Striker has massive tracks instead of wheels. The sturdy tracks are perfect for travelling on Chima's bumpy terrain.

Sharp claws
The Eagles have fitted claw-like pieces to the front of the Striker. These claws move obstacles – and enemies – out of the way.

Awesome Armour

Design new armour

All of Chima's animals wear armour. It protects them in battle, holds their CHI and shows which tribe they belong to. Lavertus, the exiled Lion, has made Laval and his friends new, stronger armour for their brave adventures in the Outlands.

Gorzan

Gorzan's Gorilla Tribe armour has huge shoulder guards, which make him look fierce. Gorzan loves nature, so his knee pads are made out of tough bark.

Read about the animals' armour. Then, design new armour for them.

The armour can be any **colour** you like.

Try creating your own new **patterns** and **decorations**.

Razcal

Razcal's armour is made up of lots of different bits of scrap metal he has pilfered from other tribes. His knee plates feature gold Raven symbols.

Laval

Laval is wearing the bigger, stronger armour built by his new friend, Lavertus. The silver chest plate is extra hard and can protect against the nastiest Scorpion stings. His knee plates feature Lions' heads.

You could use animal shapes like **bones, teeth** or **feathers**.

How would you **upgrade** the animals' armour?

Crominus

Crominus wears a royal gold chest plate to match his crown. He attaches bones to his belt. His royal cape fits over his armour, but it is tattered. Looking tidy isn't easy when you live in a swamp!

Aerial Attack

Wolf vehicles are usually **grey** and **red**.

Colour the flying vehicles

The tribes of Chima don't just fight on land – they take to the skies too. They fly into other animals' territory to steal CHI and take off in their vehicles to fend off enemy assaults.

Read about the flying vehicles. Find them in the battle scene and colour them in.

Lavertus's Twin Blade

Lavertus's helicopter is heavily armed with maCHIguns for battling the dangerous Outlands tribes. The cockpit is shaped like a Lion's head.

Braptor's Wing Striker

Braptor needs CHI to power his Wing Striker. He swoops into Chima in this Bat-like flying machine to raid Chima's CHI.

Windra's Helicopter

Windra's helicopter has huge twin spinning rotors. It's very good at quick lift-offs to chase unsuspecting enemies.

The Twin Blade is mostly **gold** with **blue** and **grey** parts.

The Wing Striker has glowing **green** eyes.

Chima Challenge

Test your knowledge on this section

Answer each question. If you need help, look back through the section.

Now you have finished the last section of the book, take the Chima Challenge to show what you have learned!

1. Find the sticker that best matches the description:

Braptor the Bat uses this winged vehicle to steal Chima's CHI.

2. Gorzan's knee pads are made from...

Scrap metal ☐   **Tree bark** ☐   **Banana skins** ☐

3. Lavertus lives in the Outlands.

True ☐   **False** ☐

4. Name this weapon. _____

5. Equila the Eagle fires _____ from each side of his Ultra Striker.

Find the **answers** on page 97.

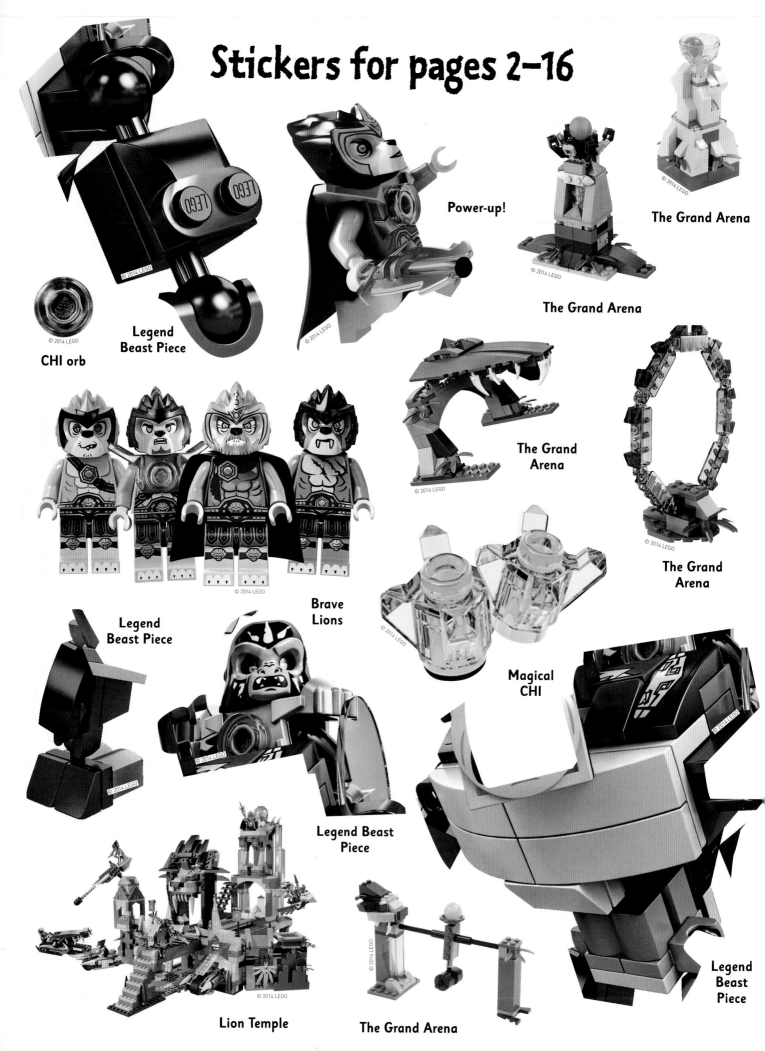

Stickers for pages 2–16

Power-up!

The Grand Arena

The Grand Arena

CHI orb

Legend Beast Piece

The Grand Arena

The Grand Arena

Brave Lions

Legend Beast Piece

Magical CHI

Legend Beast Piece

Lion Temple

The Grand Arena

Legend Beast Piece

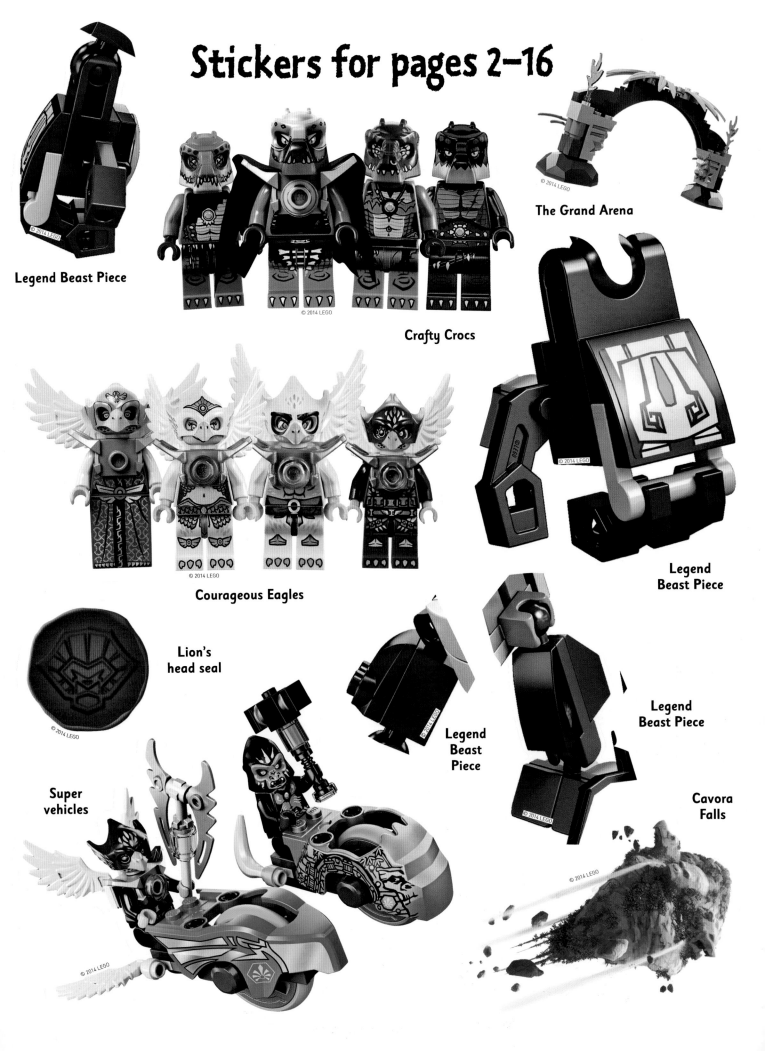

Stickers for pages 2–16

Legend Beast Piece

Crafty Crocs

The Grand Arena

Legend Beast Piece

Courageous Eagles

Lion's head seal

Legend Beast Piece

Legend Beast Piece

Super vehicles

Cavora Falls

Stickers for pages 2-16

Legend Beast Piece

Naughty Wolves

Extra stickers

© 2014 LEGO

Stickers for pages 18–32

Windra

Fighting together

The Rhino Tribe

Razcal

Rawzom

Leonidas

Leonidas escaping

Laval

Croc twins

Worriz

Longtooth

Stickers for pages 18–32

The Gorilla Tribe

Lennox

Rizzo

The bad guys

Wilhurt

Animal kings

Razar

Wakz

Combat Lair

Stickers for pages 18–32

The Raven Tribe

Friendly animals

Extra stickers

Stickers for pages 34-48

The Outlands

The Outlands

The Outlands

Scorm's Scorpion Stinger

Friend or foe?

Stolen CHI

The Outlands

Dark days

The Outlands

The Outlands

The Outlands

The Outlands

The Outlands

The Outlands

The Outlands

The Outlands

Outlands villains

Stickers for pages 34–48

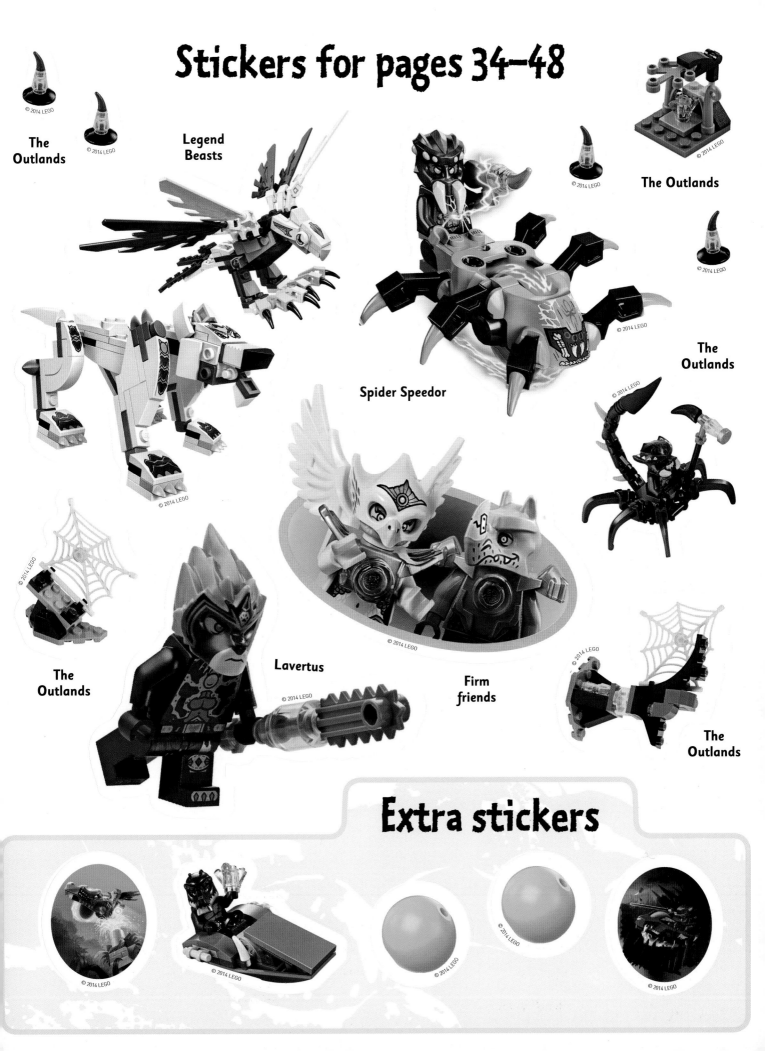

The Outlands

Legend Beasts

The Outlands

The Outlands

Spider Speedor

The Outlands

Lavertus

Firm friends

The Outlands

Extra stickers

© 2014 LEGO

Extra stickers

Extra stickers

Stickers for pages 50-64

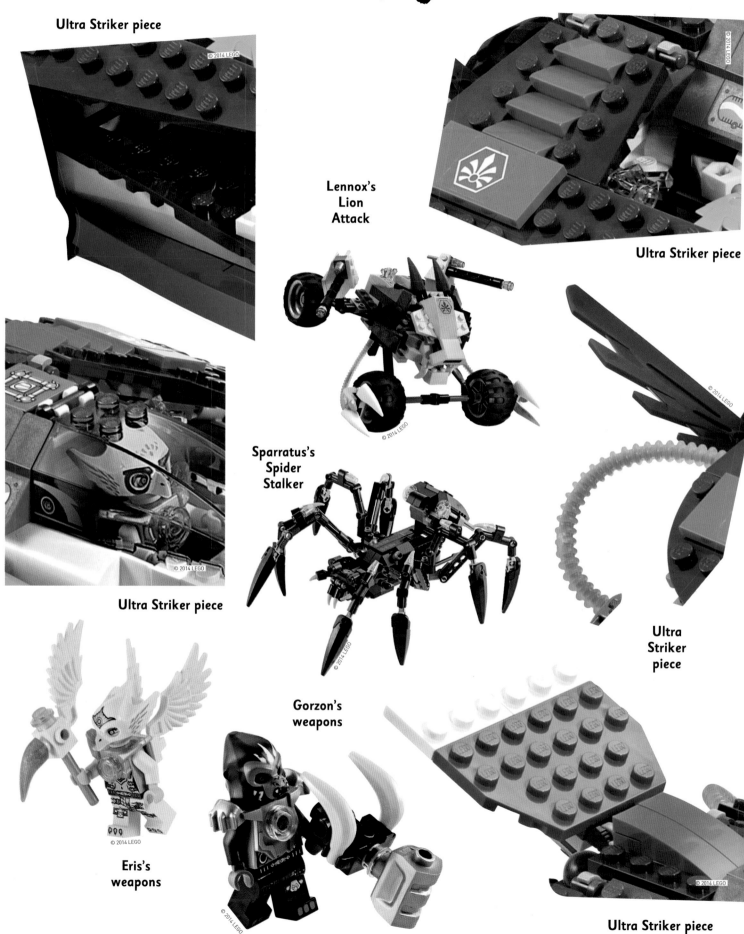

Ultra Striker piece

Lennox's Lion Attack

Ultra Striker piece

Ultra Striker piece

Sparratus's Spider Stalker

Ultra Striker piece

Gorzon's weapons

Eris's weapons

Ultra Striker piece

Stickers for pages 50-64

Ultra Striker piece

Rogon's Rock Flinger

Laval's weapons

Ultra Striker piece

Ultra Striker piece

Ultra Striker piece

Cragger's weapons

Ultra Striker piece

Stickers for pages 50-64

Ultra Striker piece

Speedorz

Braptor's Wing Striker

Extra stickers

© 2014 LEGO